A to Z of parkrun tourism

Asia Pacific

Get updates on this book and a free copy of the Runs With A Barcode transtasman parkrun tourism digital magazine by joining my mailing list.

http://eepurl.com/huE5yn

ISBN 978-0-473-57379-9

FIRST EDITION

www.runswithabarcode.co.nz

A to Z of parkrun tourism

Asia Pacific

Contents

Introduction

The first thing to consider when writing a book like this is that parkruns pop up all the time, so no sooner is it published than it is out of date.

With that in mind I will endeavour to release a new edition annually with an updated list.

In the meantime, join the Runs With A Barcode facebook group to get notifications so you can scribble in the back.

As a parkrun tourist myself, I have often scoured the parkrun website looking for which events can help me complete certain challenges.

It was while living in the UK in 2017 that I discovered there was such a thing.

I spent hours going through the global results page looking for parkruns that would enable me to complete my alphabet.

It wasn't easy as I had no idea of knowing which country they were in!

Which brings me neatly to this book.

It's Asia Pacific, rather than Australia and New Zealand, to give us some inspiration for when global travel is wide open again.

Other geographic regions are available.

I've also included when special days are celebrated so should you find yourself booking a trip to Japan, you will know when will allow you the most parkruns in the short timeframe.

Please share your adventures with me so I and others can celebrate and travel vicariously through you.

Alison King

A2147564

Facebook group: facebook.com/groups/runswithabarcodeclubhouse

Website: www.runswithabarcode.co.nz

Events listed correct as of 2/6/2021

What are the parkrun challenges?

Firstly, to caveat this, the only official parkrun challenges are the milestones for 10 (juniors only), 50, 100, 250 and 500 parkruns plus 25 volunteering occasions.

From September 1 2021 milestone shirts will be available for runners and volunteers in all colours.

The rest of the challenges you may have heard about are so unofficial that there is no recognition for completing them from parkrun itself.

However you can achieve badges on various parkrun apps, and also adoration from other parkrunners.

This list is not exhaustive.

Let me know if there's a challenge missing that you think deserves a mention so it can be considered for future editions.

Tourist - Run at 20+ different parkrun locations anywhere in the world

World Tourist - Run parkruns in at least four different countries.

Cowell Club - Run at 100+ different parkrun locations. This is named after the first parkrunners to complete it, Chris and Linda Cowell.

Cow – Run at 50 different parkrun locations. As 50 is half of 100, Cow is half of Cowell.

Freyne Club - Run at 250+ different parkrun locations. This is named after the first parkrunner to complete it, Paul Freyne.

Refreyne Club – Run at 500+ different parkrun locations, also named after Paul Freyne.

Hoffman Club – Run your first 50 parkruns at different parkrun locations (no repeats).

This is named after the first parkrunner to complete it, Roderick Hoffman.

Bailey Club – Run your first 100 parkruns at different parkrun locations (no repeats).

This is named after the first parkrunner to complete it, Gregory Bailey.

Peel Club – Run a parkrun in each Australian state and territory. This is named after the first parkrunner to achieve it, Brendan Peel.

Pioneer Club – Run the first event to start in each Australian state and territory.

Ollie Vollie – Volunteer in every Australian state and territory.

This is named after Margie Olsen, the first parkrunner to achieve this.

BrisVegas Club – Run all parkruns within the Brisbane City Council area.

Raefarers Club – Run all parkruns within the Sydney Metropolitan Area.

This is named after the first parkrunner to achieve it, Kathy Rae.

Southern Cross Stargazer Club – Originally a group of parkruns that looked like the Southern Cross constellation on the map, now expanded to include all in that particular area.

Statesman/Territorian/Countryman – Run all parkruns within a state, territory or country.

This is also known as regionnaire – run all parkruns within a defined parkrun region, such as the North Island of New Zealand.

Alphabeteer - Run at parkrun locations starting with each letter of the English alphabet (except X).

Single-Ton - Run 100+ parkruns at the same location.

Double-Ton - Run 200+ parkruns at the same location.

Stopwatch Bingo - Collect all the seconds from 00 to 59 in your finishing times.

Pirates! - Run seven Cs and an R. Variations include adding a parkrun that starts with an I and Shipwreck parkrun.

Stayin' Alive - Run three Bees and three Gees.

Bay Watch - Run all parkruns with Bay in the name.

Dizzy Heights - Run at the three highest altitude events in Australia

Compass Club - Run at a parkrun named after (or including) each of the four compass points.

Name Badge - Spell out your registered name with parkruns.

Bronze Level Obsessive - Run 30+ parkruns in one calendar year.

Silver Level Obsessive - Run 40+ parkruns in one calendar year.

Gold Level Obsessive - Run 50+ parkruns in one calendar year.

Wilson Index - relates to the highest event parkrun number that you've attended.

If you've never been to an inaugural event then your WI will be 0, if you've been to an inaugural and an event in its second week, your WI will be 2 and so on.

You can do this in any order and at any event, back-filling any gaps when you can.

P Index – The number of parkruns that satisfy the equation 'p parkruns run at least p times'.

For example, if you have run 4 different parkruns at least 4 times each, your p-index is 4.

If you have never run at an event twice, then your p-index will only be 1.

V Index - The number of volunteer roles which have been performed at least v times.

If you have volunteered in 4 different roles at least 4 times, your v-index is 4. This stat was created by Mel Erbacher on episode 158 of the *parkrun Adventurers* podcast.

There are other challenges which are not reliant on tourism. At the back of this book you can find space to plot and track your adventures.

A-Z of parkruns

In this section parkruns are broken down firstly by country and then into their regions – state, territory etc. This is to help you plan your parkrun adventures more easily.

You can also find the pilgrim events plus most easterly, southerly etc.

Tick them as you have run them so you can track your progress.

Some challenges are event specific, to track your progress for these clubs go to the next chapter.

Please note these lists do not contain parkruns that are closed to the general public (for example custodial parkruns and those on military premises), nor junior parkruns.

Before planning trips for special days make contact with the event you have in mind to avoid disappointment.

Australia

Special Event: Christmas Day

First parkrun: Main Beach (April 2, 2011)

Australian Capital Territory (ACT)

First parkrun: Ginninderra (April 28, 2012)

Burley Griffin parkrun

Coombs parkrun

Ginninderra parkrun

Gungahlin parkrun

Mount Ainslie parkrun

Tuggeranong parkrun

Wagi Bridge parkrun

New South Wales (NSW)

First parkrun: St Peters (January 21, 2012)

Albury Wodonga parkrun

Armidale parkrun

Avondale University College parkrun

Ballina Coast parkrun

Batemans Bay parkrun

Bathurst parkrun

Bega parkrun

Bill Rose Sports Complex parkrun

Blackbutt parkrun

Blue Gum Hills parkrun

Bourke Racecourse parkrun

Bowral parkrun

Braidwood Showground parkrun

Broken Hill Racecourse parkrun

Callaghan parkrun

Campbelltown parkrun

Casula Parklands parkrun

Centennial parkrun

Chipping Norton parkrun

Cobar parkrun

Coffs Harbour parkrun

Cooks River parkrun

Cowpasture Reserve parkrun, Camden

Cowra parkrun

Cronulla parkrun

Curl Curl parkrun

Dolls Point parkrun

Dubbo parkrun

East Richmond parkrun

Fingal Bay parkrun

Forster parkrun

Galston parkrun

Gloucester District parkrun

Goulburn parkrun

Grafton parkrun

GreenWay parkrun

Horseshoe Bay Reserve parkrun

Huskisson parkrun

Inverell parkrun

Jindabyne parkrun

Kamay parkrun

Kingscliff parkrun (Australia's most easterly)

Lake Mac parkrun

Lakeview parkrun

Lawson parkrun

Leeton Sport and Recreation Precinct parkrun

Lismore parkrun

Lithgow parkrun

Maitland parkrun

Menai parkrun

Merimbula parkrun

Merriwa parkrun

Moree parkrun

Mosman parkrun

Mt Penang parkrun

Mudgee parkrun

Narrabri parkrun

Narromine Wetlands parkrun

Nepean River parkrun

Newy parkrun

North Sydney parkrun

North Wollongong parkrun

Northparkes Oval parkrun

Nulkaba parkrun

Orange parkrun

Panania parkrun

Parramatta parkrun

Penrith Lakes parkrun

Picton parkrun

Pioneer Dairy parkrun

Port Macquarie parkrun

Queanbeyan parkrun

Queen Elizabeth parkrun, Casino

Rhodes parkrun

Riverbank parkrun

Rooty Hill parkrun

San Remo parkrun

Sandon Point parkrun

Shellharbour parkrun

Singleton parkrun

St Peters parkrun

Stockton parkrun

Tamworth parkrun

Taree parkrun

Ted Scobie Oval parkrun

The Beaches parkrun

The Entrance parkrun

The Ponds parkrun

The Terrace parkrun

Urunga parkrun

Wagga parkrun

Walcha parkrun

Wauchope parkrun

Werrington Lakes Reserve parkrun

Whalan Reserve parkrun

Wildflower parkrun

Willoughby parkrun

Woy Woy parkrun

Yamba parkrun

Northern Territory (NT)

First parkrun: Darwin (October 26, 2013)

Darwin parkrun

Nightcliff parkrun (Australia's most northerly)

Palmerston parkrun

Queensland (QLD)

First parkrun: Main Beach (April 2, 2011)

Airlie Beach parkrun

Aplins Weir parkrun

Ashgrove parkrun

Atherton parkrun

Bargara parkrun

Baringa parkrun

Berrinba parkrun

Bowen parkrun

Brightwater parkrun

Broadbeach Waters parkrun

Bundaberg parkrun

Bunyaville parkrun

Cairns parkrun

Calamvale parkrun

Capalaba parkrun

Cardwell parkrun

Centenary parkrun

Central Lakes parkrun

Charleys Creek parkrun

Chermside parkrun

Cleveland parkrun

Cloncurry parkrun

Coomera parkrun

Cormorant Bay parkrun

Dalby parkrun

Emerald parkrun

Forest Lake parkrun

Gainsborough Greens parkrun

Gatton parkrun

Gayndah River Walk parkrun

Gladstone QLD parkrun

Glass House Mountains Conservation parkrun

Golden Beach parkrun

Goondiwindi parkrun

Graham Andrews parkrun

Greenbank parkrun

Hamilton Island parkrun

Harris Avenue parkrun

Hervey Bay parkrun

Highfields parkrun

Ipswich QLD parkrun

Kawana parkrun

Kedron parkrun

Kelvin Grove parkrun

Kirra parkrun

Logan River parkrun

Lota parkrun

Mackay parkrun

Main Beach parkrun

Maleny Trail parkrun

Mansfield parkrun, Queensland

Maryborough parkrun

Meadowbrook parkrun

Miles parkrun

Minnippi parkrun

Mitchelton parkrun

Mount Isa parkrun

Mudgeeraba parkrun

Mudjimba Beach parkrun

Nambour parkrun

New Farm parkrun

Noosa parkrun

North Harbour parkrun

North Lakes parkrun

North Shore parkrun

Oakey parkrun

Ocean View parkrun

Old Thomson River Road parkrun

Pallara parkrun

Paradise Point parkrun

Petrie parkrun

Pittsworth parkrun

Plantation parkrun

Redcliffe parkrun

Redland Bay parkrun

Riverway parkrun

Rockhampton parkrun

Rocks Riverside parkrun

Roma parkrun

Ros Gregor Trail parkrun

S.S. Koopa Trail parkrun

Sandgate parkrun

Sirromet parkrun

South Bank parkrun

South Toowoomba parkrun

St George parkrun

St Lucia parkrun

Stanthorpe parkrun

Stones Corner parkrun (check if re-opened after course works)

Surfers Paradise parkrun

Tamborine Mountain parkrun

Tannum Sands parkrun

Toowoomba parkrun

TYTO Wetlands parkrun

Underwood Park parkrun

Varsity Lakes parkrun

Victory Heights Trail parkrun

Warner Lakes parkrun

Warwick parkrun

Waterloo Plains parkrun

Weipa parkrun

White Rock parkrun

Wishart parkrun

Wondai parkrun

Wynnum parkrun

Yarrabilba parkrun

Yeppoon parkrun

Yowie parkrun

Zillmere parkrun

South Australia (SA)

First parkrun: Torrens (December 1, 2012)

Aldinga Beach parkrun

Carisbrooke parkrun

Charleston parkrun, South Australia

Christies Beach parkrun

Clare Valley parkrun

Cleland parkrun

Edithburgh parkrun

Gawler parkrun

Goolwa parkrun

Jubilee Way parkrun

Kangaroo Island parkrun

Largs Bay parkrun

Lochiel parkrun

Mawson Lakes parkrun

Meningie parkrun

Moana parkrun

Mount Barker parkrun

Mount Gambier parkrun

Murray Bridge parkrun

Naracoorte Lake parkrun

Nuriootpa parkrun

Pakapakanthi parkrun

Port Augusta parkrun

Port Broughton parkrun

Port Lincoln parkrun

Renmark parkrun

Reynella East parkrun

Seacliff Esplanade parkrun

Shiraz Trail parkrun

Stebonheath parkrun

Strathalbyn parkrun

The Avenues

Torrens parkrun

Victor Harbor parkrun

West Beach parkrun

Yeldulknie Weir Trail parkrun

Tasmania (TAS)

First parkrun: Launceston (November 10, 2012)

Bellerive parkrun

Burnie parkrun

Devonport parkrun

Geeveston parkrun (Australia's most southerly parkrun)

George Town parkrun

Kate Reed parkrun

Kingston Park parkrun

Launceston parkrun

Montrose Foreshore parkrun

Our Park parkrun

Port Sorell parkrun

Queens Domain parkrun

Railton parkrun

Risdon Brook parkrun

Whitemark Wharf parkrun

Windsor Precinct parkrun

Wynyard Foreshore parkrun

Victoria (VIC)

First parkrun: Albert (November 19, 2011)

Albert parkrun, Melbourne

Altona Beach parkrun

Ararat parkrun

Aurora parkrun

Bairnsdale parkrun

Ballarat parkrun

Balyang Sanctuary parkrun

Bannockburn Bush parkrun

Benalla Botanical Gardens parkrun

Bendigo Botanic Gardens parkrun

Bendigo parkrun

Berwick Springs parkrun

Berwick Waters parkrun

Birdsland Reserve parkrun

Bright parkrun

Brimbank parkrun

Campaspe parkrun

Cascades on Clyde Wetlands parkrun

Castlemaine parkrun

Chelsea Bicentennial parkrun

Churchill parkrun

Cobram parkrun

Coburg parkrun

Cohuna parkrun

Dandenong parkrun

Darebin parkrun

Diamond Creek parkrun

Eastern Gardens parkrun

Echuca Moama parkrun

Euroa parkrun

Fairpark Reserve parkrun

Frog Hollow parkrun

Gardiners Creek parkrun

Goldfields Reservoir parkrun

Grand Ridge Rail Trail parkrun, Mirboo North

Hamilton parkrun

Hastings Foreshore parkrun

Highlands parkrun

Inverloch parkrun

Jells parkrun

Karkarook parkrun

Kennington Reservoir parkrun

Kerang Regional parkrun

KM Reedy Reserve parkrun

Koonwarra parkrun

Lake Boga Foreshore parkrun

Lakes Entrance parkrun

Lalor parkrun

Lancefield parkrun

Lillydale Lake parkrun

Lorne Beach parkrun

Louis Hamon Park parkrun

Mansfield Botanic parkrun

Maribyrnong parkrun

Marriott Waters parkrun

Mernda parkrun

Mildura Weir parkrun

Mount Beauty parkrun

Mullum Mullum parkrun

Newborough parkrun

Newport Lakes parkrun

Nhill parkrun

Ocean Grove parkrun

Ovens River Trail parkrun

Pakenham parkrun

Parkville parkrun

Peppertree parkrun

Phillip Island parkrun

Point Cook parkrun

Port Fairy parkrun

Portarlington parkrun

Portland parkrun

Rosebud parkrun

Sale parkrun

Shepparton parkrun

Studley parkrun

Sunbury parkrun

Timboon parkrun

Toolern Creek parkrun

Torquay parkrun

Traralgon parkrun

Wallaby Track parkrun

Wangaratta parkrun

Warragul parkrun

Warringal Parklands parkrun

Warrnambool parkrun

Westerfolds parkrun

Williamstown Breakwater parkrun

Willow parkrun

Wilson Botanic parkrun

Wimmera River parkrun, Horsham

Wyndham Vale parkrun

You Yangs parkrun

Western Australia (WA)

First parkrun: Claisebrook Cove (August 4, 2012)

Applecross parkrun

Aveley parkrun

Bibra Lake parkrun

Bunbury parkrun

Burswood Peninsula parkrun

Calleya parkrun

Canning River parkrun

Carine Glades parkrun

Champion Lakes parkrun

Claisebrook Cove parkrun

Collie River Trail parkrun

Cottesloe parkrun

Dawesville parkrun

Edinburgh Oval parkrun

Garvey Park parkrun

Geographe Bay parkrun

Hampton Oval parkrun

Kadina Trail parkrun

Kalgoorlie-Boulder parkrun

Kununurra parkrun

Lake Joondalup parkrun

Manjimup parkrun

Margaret River parkrun

Marina parkrun (Australia's most westerly parkrun)

Maylands Peninsula parkrun

Moora parkrun

Mount Helena parkrun

Mt Clarence parkrun

Mundy Regional parkrun

Perry Lakes parkrun

Pioneer parkrun

Port Hedland parkrun

Quinns Rocks parkrun

Rockingham parkrun

Shelley parkrun

Shipwreck parkrun

Tamworth Wetlands parkrun

Wanneroo parkrun

Whitfords Nodes parkrun

Woodbridge Riverside parkrun

Yokine parkrun

Japan

Special Event: Greenery Day, May 4.

The first Greenery Day was originally on April 29, 1989. It replaced the public holiday known as Birthday of the Emperor (Hirohito, known as Emperor Showa).

In 2007 it was moved to May 4 and April 29 was renamed Showa Day.

First parkrun: Futakotamagawa parkrun (April 6, 2019)

Fukakitaryokuchi parkrun

Futakotamagawa parkrun

Hikarigaoka koen parkrun

Hirono kaigankoen parkrun

Hondajima parkrun

Horinouchi koen parkrun

Kariyashi sogoundo koen parkrun

Kashiwanoha parkrun (most easterly)

Maborikaigan yuhodo parkrun

Meijo koen parkrun

Momoi harappa koen parkrun

Nagaragawa koen parkrun

Odakaryokuchi parkrun

Oiso undokoen parkrun

Oyodogawa shiminryokuchi parkrun (most southerly and western)

Sanukikodomonokuni parkrun

Shimanami Earthland parkrun

Shirahama koen parkrun

Tamagawa chou koen parkrun

Tsujido kaihin koen parkrun

Urayasushi sogo koen parkrun

Wataraseyusuichi parkrun (most northerly)

Yodogawa kasenkoen Hirakata chiku parkrun

Malaysia

Special Event: Malaysia Day, September 16. This day celebrates the establishment of the Malaysian federation in 1963.

First parkrun: Taman Pudu Ulu parkrun (April 14 2018)

Presint 18 parkrun, Putrajaya (most southerly)

Taman Pudu Ulu parkrun (most northerly)

New Zealand

Special Event: Christmas Day

First parkrun: Lower Hutt parkrun (May 5, 2012)

North Island

Anderson parkrun

Barry Curtis parkrun

Cambridge NZ parkrun

Cornwall Park parkrun

East End parkrun, New Plymouth

Flaxmere parkrun

Gisborne parkrun (New Zealand and Global most easterly)

Greytown Woodside Trail parkrun

Hamilton Lake parkrun

Hobsonville Point parkrun

Kapiti Coast parkrun

Lower Hutt parkrun

Millwater parkrun

Owairaka parkrun

Palmerston North parkrun

Porirua parkrun

Puarenga parkrun

Taupo parkrun

Tauranga parkrun

Trentham Memorial parkrun

University of Waikato parkrun

Western Springs parkrun

Whanganui Riverbank parkrun

Whangarei parkrun (New Zealand's most northerly)

South Island

Balclutha parkrun

Blenheim parkrun

Dunedin parkrun

Foster parkrun

Hagley parkrun

Invercargill parkrun (New Zealand's most southerly and westerly)

Pegasus parkrun

Queenstown parkrun

Wanaka parkrun

Singapore

Special Event: National Day of Singapore, August 9. This day celebrates independence from Malaysia in 1965.

First parkrun: East Coast Park parkrun (June 21, 2014)

Bedok Reservoir parkrun (most easterly)

Bishan parkrun (most northerly)

East Coast Park parkrun (most southerly)

West Coast Park parkrun (most westerly)

Which parkrun for which challenge?

Chasing a particular challenge? This chapter will hopefully help you plan your parkrundays.

Again, please note that as new parkruns start up this list is not definitive, which is why there's space for you to fill in names of new events.

Tick off the parkruns as you run them, there's more scribble space at the back of the book to plan your parkrun adventures.

For non-geographic specific challenges (such as Pirates), I have listed all parkruns in the Asia-Pacific region.

BrisVegas

All parkruns in the Brisbane City Council area

Ashgrove parkrun

Bunyaville parkrun

Calamvale parkrun

Chermside parkrun

Forest Lake parkrun

Kedron parkrun

Kelvin Grove parkrun

Lota parkrun

Mansfield parkrun, Queensland

Minnippi parkrun

Mitchelton parkrun

New Farm parkrun

Pallara parkrun

Rocks Riverside parkrun

Sandgate parkrun

South Bank parkrun

St Lucia parkrun

Wishart parkrun

Wynnum parkrun

Zillmere parkrun

Raefarer

All parkruns in the Sydney Metropolitan area

Campbelltown parkrun

Casula Parklands parkrun

Centennial Park parkrun

Chipping Norton parkrun

Cooks River parkrun

Cowpasture Reserve parkrun, Camden

Cronulla parkrun

Curl Curl parkrun

Dolls Point parkrun

East Richmond parkrun

Galston parkrun

Greenway parkrun

Kamay parkrun

Menai parkrun

Mosman parkrun

Nepean River parkrun

North Sydney parkrun

Panania parkrun

Parramatta parkrun

Penrith Lakes parkrun

Rhodes parkrun

Rooty Hill parkrun

Rouse Hill parkrun

St Peters parkrun

The Ponds parkrun

Werrington Lakes parkrun

Wildflower parkrun

Whalan Reserve

Willoughby parkrun

Stargazer

Originally a group of parkruns that looked like the Southern Cross constellation on the map, now expanded to include all in that particular area.

Original

Gatton parkrun

Highfields parkrun

Pittsworth parkrun

South Toowoomba parkrun

Stanthorpe parkrun

Toowoomba parkrun

Warwick parkrun

Bonus

Dalby parkrun

Goondwindi parkrun

Miles parkrun

Oakley parkrun

Roma parkrun

St George parkrun

Pioneer Club

The first event in each Australian state and territory.

Ginninderra (ACT)

St Peters (NSW)

Darwin (NT)

Main Beach (QLD)

Torrens (SA)

Launceston (TAS)

Albert (VIC)

Claisebrook Cove (WA)

Pirates

All in Australia unless marked

Cairns parkrun

Calamvale parkrun

Callaghan parkrun

Calleya parkrun

Cambridge NZ parkrun New Zealand

Campapse parkrun

Campbelltown parkrun

Canning River parkrun

Capalaba parkrun

Cardwell parkrun

Carine Glades parkrun

Carisbrooke parkrun

Cascades on Clyde Wetlands parkrun

Castlemaine parkrun

Centennial parkrun

Central Lakes parkrun

Champion Lakes parkrun

Charleston parkrun, South Australia

Charleys Creek parkrun

Chelsea Bicentennial parkrun

Chermside parkrun

Chipping Norton parkrun

Christies Beach parkrun

Churchill parkrun

Claisebrook Cove parkrun

Clare Valley parkrun

Cleland parkrun

Cleveland parkrun

Cloncurry parkrun

Cobar parkrun

Cobram parkrun

Coburg parkrun

Coffs Harbour parkrun

Cohuna parkrun

Collie River Trail parkrun

Cooks River parkrun

Coombs parkrun

Coomera parkrun

Cormorant Bay parkrun

Cornwall Park parkrun New Zealand

Cottesloe parkrun

Cowpasture Reserve parkrun, Camden

Cowra parkrun

Cronulla parkrun

Curl Curl parkrun

Railton parkrun

Redcliffe parkrun

Redland Bay parkrun

Renmark parkrun

Reynella East parkrun

Rhodes parkrun

Riverbank parkrun

Riverway parkrun

Rockhampton parkrun

Rocks Riverside parkrun

Roma parkrun

Rooty Hill parkrun

Ros Gregor Trail parkrun

Rosebud parkrun

Rouse Hill parkrun

Stayin' Alive

All in Australia unless marked

B

Bairnsdale parkrun

Balclutha parkrun New Zealand

Ballarat parkrun

Ballina Coast parkrun

Balyang Sanctuary parkrun

Banksia Hill parkrun

Bannockburn Bush parkrun

Bargara parkrun

Baringa parkrun

Barry Curtis parkrun New Zealand

Batemans Bay parkrun

Bathurst parkrun

Bega parkrun

Bellerive parkrun

Bellevue Park junior parkrun

Benalla Botanical Gardens parkrun

Bendigo Botanic Gardens parkrun

Bendigo parkrun

Berrinba parkrun

Berwick Springs parkrun

Berwick Waters parkrun

Bibra Lake parkrun

Bill Rose Sports Complex parkrun

Birdsland Reserve parkrun

Blackbutt parkrun

Blenheim parkrun New Zealand

Blue Gum Hills parkrun

Bourke Racecourse parkrun

Bowen parkrun

Bowral parkrun

Braidwood Showground parkrun

Bright parkrun

Brightwater parkrun

Brimbank parkrun

Broadbeach Waters parkrun

Broken Hill parkrun

Broken Hill Racecourse parkrun

Bunbury parkrun

Bundaberg parkrun

Bunyaville parkrun

Burley Griffin parkrun

Burnie parkrun

Burswood Peninsula parkrun

G

Gainsborough Greens parkrun

Galston parkrun

Gardiners Creek parkrun

Garvey Park parkrun

Gatton parkrun

Gawler parkrun

Gayndah River Walk parkrun

Geeveston parkrun

Geographe Bay parkrun

George Town parkrun

Ginninderra parkrun

Gisborne parkrun New Zealand

Gladstone QLD parkrun

Glass House Mountains Conservation parkrun

Gloucester District parkrun

Golden Beach parkrun

Goldfields Reservoir parkrun

Goolwa parkrun

Goondiwindi parkrun

Goulburn parkrun

Grafton parkrun

Graham Andrews parkrun

Grand Ridge Rail Trail parkrun, Mirboo North

Greenbank parkrun

GreenWay parkrun

Greytown Woodside Trail parkrun New Zealand

Gungahlin parkrun

Bay Watch

Australia only

Batemans Bay

Cormorant Bay

Fingal Bay

Geographe Bay

Hervey Bay

Horseshoe Bay Reserve

Largs Bay

Redland Bay

Dizzy Heights Australia

Three highest altitude events in Australia

Armidale

Lithgow

Orange

Compass Club

All in Australia unless marked

Charleston parkrun, South Australia

East Coast Park parkrun (Singapore)

East End parkrun, New Plymouth New Zealand

East Richmond parkrun

Eastern Gardens parkrun

Grand Ridge Rail Trail parkrun, Mirboo North

North Harbour parkrun

North Lakes parkrun

North Shore parkrun

North Sydney parkrun

North Wollongong parkrun

Northparkes Oval parkrun

Palmerston North parkrun New Zealand

Reynella East parkrun

South Bank parkrun

South Toowoomba parkrun

West Beach parkrun

West Coast Park parkrun (Singapore)

Westerfolds parkrun

Western Springs parkrun New Zealand

parkrun tourism planning

If parkrun tourism is new to you, or you only have a few different events under your belt, this all might seem a bit much right now.

Here is a mini course to help you get started.

This mini-course outline is broken into three primary lessons:

- Where you are now
- Where you can go next
- How to make the most of it

Lesson 1: Where You Are Now

We'll start at the very beginning. Your parkrun barcode is your ticket to any parkrun that is open if you can get to it.

There are several resources available to parkrunners to help get more from their barcode than a weekly run and result.

This can lead to weekends away or even holiday planning around parkrun and where you can run on a Saturday morning.

Download the Running Achievements and 5km apps (the latter is purple with a white runner).

These store all your parkrun results and can show you a whole range of information and stats on those you have already run, including your nearest parkrun not yet run (known as NENDY).

This site is helpful if you are travelling to a place where you have no idea if they have parkrun or not.

There are lots of facebook groups for parkrun tourists, some are specific to a region, such as Sydney, some are Australia or New Zealand wide.

Task: Use these tools to discover your NENDY (nearest event not done yet) and to look up a dream holiday destination to see if parkrun exists near there.

Lesson 2: Why Tour and Where To Next

Now that we have the apps you can now find out where your NENDY parkrun is.

Your nearest event not done yet can be a good place to start with parkrun tourism unless you are already booked on a trip away and the tourist tool showed a parkrun nearby.

Before we go into the next stage I want to give you some ways how parkrun tourism can be good for you.

For many parkrunners Saturday morning as the same routine. They get up, they go to their local event and they go home.

Now there's nothing wrong in doing this and becoming a passionista[1]. This is a great way to become fully entrenched in your local community.

However, parkrun tourism has a number of positives.

---

[1] A passionista is a parkrunner who runs only (or at least mostly) at their home event.

- It can help us to appreciate the event we have at home, so when we return we take the opportunity to get to know more of our fellow parkrunners.
- It can give us ideas on how we can improve our home event - especially if you are one of the volunteers. Even though parkruns are all free and 5km, each event team has their own unique way of staging them.
- It gives us the opportunity to explore other parts of our country while remaining active.
- It gives us the opportunity to meet the locals while on holiday and get to know the secret spots that only locals know (the best coffee, best places to eat, best beaches etc).

So now you know where you're going next, here's how to start planning.

Each event has it's own page on the parkrun website.

In New Zealand they are parkrun.co.nz/eventname, in Australia it's parkrun.com.au/eventname.

If you're in New Zealand then also check out www.runswithabarcode.co.nz/nz-events. You can find each parkrun in NZ with information from the course pages as well as more information.

Task: Look up your chosen event and start planning.

If it's your NENDY can you drive to it in the morning, or do you need to book an overnight stay?

When can you visit? Fix a date as soon as you can.

Lesson 3: How To Make The Most Of Your Trip

I've visited so many parkruns where afterwards I felt disappointed in myself for not knowing what else there was to see and do while I was there.

Some visits have been a run and go home, which has left me wanting to return and spend more time in the location.

But other visits have been jam-packed with activities and options that have made the trip feel so worth the hours in the car - and in need of another holiday to get over this one!

What you get out of your parkrun tourism all depends on what you put into it.

Some parkruns are only a short drive away so you may end up returning more often and exploring in more detail.

But those that require a bit of effort (such as an overnight stay or long early drive) deserve reward for that.

Now you know where you're going and whether you need to stay this is where you can start planning.

Firstly where to stay?

I either ask other tourists where they stayed or generally use google, ideally looking for accommodation thatoffers free cancellation.

If you are driving then being as close as possible to the start isn't key, but being within a couple of kilometres will allow for a cruisy morning.

Next, what else can you do while down there?

If you're looking up a New Zealand course then my website will give you some suggestions.

Next Google "Things to do in" with where you are going to see what comes recommended.

If you have any preference for activities then google that phrase with where you're at, eg walking tracks near xx, craft beer near xx.

Look up places to eat too, are there any markets or food trucks you simply must visit?

Don't forget the value of parkrun tourism facebook groups.

Keep a note of everything that you discover and then start to plan a rough itinerary.

If there are any activities or restaurants that are must-dos then see if there are any deals you can take advantage of.

The week of your parkrun trip message the parkrun you are visiting and let them know you are coming along and where from.

This is an opportunity to ask them if they have any recommendations for things to do in their area, or maybe ask where is a good place to eat on Friday night.

Visit their facebook page to see if they are having a special dress-up occasion, so you can be prepared, or in case of cancellation.

Visit their parkrun webpage for parking, start location, toilets and start time.

Locals know their area best, and this leads to my favourite tip.

Talk to the locals at parkrun, either chat to the volunteers after you've finished or (definitely) go to the cafe venue afterwards so you can learn other places that you must see.

The night before your parkrun adventure make sure you know where you're going and have a plan for how to get there.

If you have the opportunity, do a practice run, so there are no surprises on the morning.

And most of all, **don't forget your barcode**.

Arrive with plenty of time to attend a first timers' briefing, if the event holds one, or to chat with a volunteer to familiarise yourself with the course.

What Happens Next?

Please share your parkrun adventures in the www.facebook.com/groups/runswithabarcodeclubhouse group. You may just inspire another parkrunner to visit.

Building a relationship with readers is the best thing about writing.

As well as these tourism-related books I write blogs and produce a monthly digital magazine full of parkrunners and their events.

You can get a free copy of this magazine by joining my mailing list.

This is where I'll let you know about updates to this edition and when new titles are published.

You'll get all this by signing up here:

http://eepurl.com/huE5yn

Enjoyed this book?

You can make a difference.

Honest reviews of my books help bring them to the attention of other readers.

If you've found this book helpful I'd be very grateful if you could take a few minutes on the book's Amazon page.

Thank you very much!

Acknowledgements

A special thanks to all parkrun tourists everywhere who have documented their travels.

I'd like to give extra thanks to Peter Pohlman and his Australian parkrun spreadsheet.

To the With Me Now patreon group for letting me know of other apps and challenges.

parkrun Adventurers, for inspiring this book. I can't wait to be able to spend a lot more time on the West Island visiting parkruns.

And to parkrun tourists everywhere who talk of Wilson Index, Pirates and Stopwatch Bingo as if it were common knowledge.

You are my kind of people!

Tracking Your Challenges

Fill this in as you complete your parkruns so you can check while away from your spreadsheets.

Alphabet

A

B

C

D

E

F

G

H

I

J

K

L

M

N

O

P

Q

R

S

T

U

V

W

Y

Z

Wilson Index

1

2

3

4

5

6

7

8

9

10

11

12

13

14

15

16

85

86

87

88

89

90

91

92

93

94

95

96

97

98

99

100

Pirates

C

C

C

C

C

C

C

R

Compass Club

North

East

South

West

Stayin' Alive

B

G

B

G

B

G

Peel Club

ACT

NSW

NT

QLD

SA

TAS

VIC

WA

Pioneer Club

Ginninderra (ACT)

St Peters (NSW)

Darwin (NT)

Main Beach (QLD)

Torrens (SA)

Launceston (TAS)

Albert (VIC)

Claisebrook Cove (WA)

Volunteer Roles

Tick these off as you volunteer

Equipment Storage and Delivery

Communications Person

Volunteer Co-ordinator

Event Day Course Check

Pre-event Setup

Car Park Marshal

First Timers Briefing

Warm Up Leader (junior parkrun)

Sign Language Support

Marshal

Tail Walker

Run Director

Lead Bike

Pacer

Guide Runner

Photographer

Timer

Funnel Manager

Finish Tokens & Support

Barcode Scanning

Number Checker

Post-event Close Down

Results Processor

Token Sorting

Run Report Writer

Other

Planning Space

www.ingramcontent.com/pod-product-compliance
Ingram Content Group UK Ltd.
Pitfield, Milton Keynes, MK11 3LW, UK
UKHW021050270726
13967UKWH00012B/198

9 780473 573799